MOSINEE PROJECT

by Counterfactual

SAMUEL FRENCH

Copyright © 2024 by Counterfactual
Artwork design: Guy J Sanders
All Rights Reserved

THE MOSINEE PROJECT is fully protected under the copyright laws of the British Commonwealth, including Canada, the United States of America, and all other countries of the Copyright Union. All rights, including professional and amateur stage productions, recitation, lecturing, public reading, motion picture, radio broadcasting, television, online/digital production, and the rights of translation into foreign languages are strictly reserved.

ISBN 978-0-573-00064-5

concordtheatricals.co.uk
concordtheatricals.com

FOR AMATEUR PRODUCTION ENQUIRIES

UNITED KINGDOM AND WORLD
EXCLUDING NORTH AMERICA
licensing@concordtheatricals.co.uk
020-7054-7298

Each title is subject to availability from Concord Theatricals, depending upon country of performance.

CAUTION: Professional and amateur producers are hereby warned that *THE MOSINEE PROJECT* is subject to a licensing fee. The purchase, renting, lending or use of this book does not constitute a licence to perform this title(s), which licence must be obtained from the appropriate agent prior to any performance. Performance of this title(s) without a licence is a violation of copyright law and may subject the producer and/or presenter of such performances to penalties. Both amateurs and professionals considering a production are strongly advised to apply to the appropriate agent before starting rehearsals, advertising, or booking a theatre. A licensing fee must be paid whether the title is presented for charity or gain and whether or not admission is charged.

This work is published by Samuel French, an imprint of Concord Theatricals Ltd.

To inquire about Professional Rights, contact Concord Theatricals.

No one shall make any changes in this title for the purpose of production. No part of this book may be reproduced, stored in a retrieval system, scanned, uploaded, or transmitted in any form, by any means, now known or yet to be invented, including mechanical, electronic, digital, photocopying, recording, videotaping, or otherwise, without the prior written permission of the publisher. No one shall share this title, or part of this title, to any social media or file hosting websites.

The moral right of Counterfactual to be identified as author of this work has been asserted in accordance with Section 77 of the Copyright, Designs and Patents Act 1988.

USE OF COPYRIGHTED MUSIC

A licence issued by Concord Theatricals to perform this play does not include permission to use the incidental music specified in this publication. In the United Kingdom: Where the place of performance is already licensed by the PERFORMING RIGHT SOCIETY (PRS) a return of the music used must be made to them. If the place of performance is not so licensed then application should be made to PRS for Music (www.prsformusic.com). A separate and additional licence from PHONOGRAPHIC PERFORMANCE LTD (www.ppluk.com) may be needed whenever commercial recordings are used. Outside the United Kingdom: Please contact the appropriate music licensing authority in your territory for the rights to any incidental music.

USE OF COPYRIGHTED THIRD-PARTY MATERIALS

Licensees are solely responsible for obtaining formal written permission from copyright owners to use copyrighted third-party materials (e.g., artworks, logos) in the performance of this play and are strongly cautioned to do so. If no such permission is obtained by the licensee, then the licensee must use only original materials that the licensee owns and controls. Licensees are solely responsible and liable for clearances of all third-party copyrighted materials, and shall indemnify the copyright owners of the play(s) and their licensing agent, Concord Theatricals Ltd., against any costs, expenses, losses and liabilities arising from the use of such copyrighted third-party materials by licensees.

IMPORTANT BILLING AND CREDIT REQUIREMENTS

If you have obtained performance rights to this title, please refer to your licensing agreement for important billing and credit requirements.

NOTE

This edition reflects a rehearsal draft of the script and may differ from the final production.

THE MOSINEE PROJECT was first produced by New Diorama Theatre, and premiered at Underbelly at the Edinburgh Fringe on 1 August 2024. The cast and creative team were as follows:

JOHN DECKER/
MAYOR RALPH E KRONENWETTER .... Jonathan Oldfield
BENJAMIN GITLOW/
FRANCIS SCHWEINLER .... Martha Watson Allpress
JOSEPH ZACK KORNFEDER .... Millicent Wong

Writer/Director .... Nikhil Vyas
Original Co-Creator/Dramaturg .... Aaron Kilercioglu
Co-Creators and performers .... Jonathan Oldfield, Martha Watson Allpress, Millicent Wong
Additional Material .... Martha Watson Allpress, Breffni Holahan, Jessica Layde, Jonathan Oldfield

Set and Costume Designer .... Grace Venning
Lighting Designer .... Catja Hamilton
Sound Designer .... Patch Middleton
Video System Designer .... Dan Light
Research Consultant .... Emma Jude Harris
Producer .... Jessie Anand
Stage Manager .... Josh Trackman

Supported using public funding by the National Lottery through Arts Council England, with additional support from MGCfutures and the Unity Theatre Trust.

New Diorama Theatre

New Diorama Theatre is a pioneering studio venue in the heart of London.

Based on the corner of Regent's Park, over the last ten years New Diorama has been at the heart of a new movement in British theatre. New Diorama is the only venue in the UK entirely dedicated to providing a home for the country's best independent theatre companies and ensembles, and has established a national record as a trailblazer for early-career artist support.

"A genuine theatrical phenomenon – a miniature powerhouse." – *The Stage*

In 2022, New Diorama was named *The Stage*'s Fringe Theatre Of The Year, for the second time in its short history; and in 2023 was awarded the inaugural Critics' Circle Empty Space Venue Award. Since opening in 2010, New Diorama's work has also won four prestigious Peter Brook Awards; eleven Off West End Awards including Off West End Artistic Director of the Year; and *The Stage*'s Innovation Prize.

"A must-visit destination for London theatregoers." – *Time Out*

Work commissioned and produced at New Diorama frequently tours nationally and internationally, including regular transfers Off Broadway and co-curating New York's celebrated Brits Off Broadway Festival with 59E59 Theaters. *The Stage* 100, which charts power and influence across British Theatre, currently list New Diorama as the most influential independent studio theatre in the UK.

"A crucial part of the wider UK theatre ecology and an under-sung hero." – *The Guardian*

In 2023, New Diorama achieved a further milestone with two original commissions transferring into London's West End. *For Black Boys Who Have Considered Suicide When The Hue Gets Too Heavy*, originally co-produced with Nouveau Riche and earning their artistic director Ryan Calais-Cameron an Olivier Award nomination for Best New Play, transferred first to the Royal Court Theatre before sell-out West End runs at the Apollo Theatre and Garrick Theatre. Alongside, *Operation Mincemeat*, an original New Diorama commission from musical theatre company Spitlip, transferred to the Fortune Theatre, where it is currently playing an open-ended run after multiple extensions and has won the 2024 Olivier Award for Best New Musical.

"New Diorama has only been around for a decade but has already left a huge mark on the global theatre scene." – *WhatsOnStage*

www.newdiorama.com | @NewDiorama | New Diorama Theatre, 15-16 Triton Street, Regent's Place, London NW1 3BF.

underbelly

Established in 2000, Underbelly is a UK-based live entertainment company specialising in programming and producing groundbreaking theatrical productions, cultural city centre events and original festivals.

Founded at the Edinburgh Festival Fringe by Ed Bartlam and Charlie Wood, Underbelly remains a pioneer of untapped talent across the world of theatre, comedy, circus and cabaret, entertaining audiences from London to Edinburgh, and Asia to North America.

As a leading venue producer at the Edinburgh Festival Fringe, Underbelly's 2024 programme will welcome over 160+ shows across 20 performances spaces. Notable highlights across our 24-year history at the festival include Phoebe Waller-Bridge's *Fleabag* in 2013, Marlow and Moss' *SIX* in 2018, Manual Cinema's *Ada/Ava* in 2016, 1927's *Between the Devil and the Deep Blue Sea* in 2007, Rob Madge's *My Son's A Queer (But What Can You Do?)* in 2022 and Francesca Moody Productions' *Kathy & Stella Solve a Murder!* in 2023.

On the West End, Underbelly is the lead and originating producer of the Olivier Award-winning revival of *Cabaret* at the Kit Kat Club, alongside ATG Productions, now in its third year and originally starring Eddie Redmayne and Jessie Buckley.

Expanding into new ventures, in 2023 Underbelly launched its first permanent venue, Underbelly Boulevard, in the heart of Soho. A vibrant and dynamic entertainment destination boasting a state-of-the-art auditorium, Underbelly Boulevard has hosted world-class cabaret, comedy, theatre and circus in its inaugural year including Bernie Dieter's *Club Kabarett*; Three Legged Race Productions' *Sophie's Surprise 29th*; John Bishop; Josh Thomas; Mason Alexander Park's *The Pansy Craze*; and Mario The Maker Magician.

Other current London festivals include Underbelly Festival at Cavendish Square, Christmas in Leicester Square and Christmas in Trafalgar Square; as well as proudly being the event production partner for West End Live in Trafalgar Square (on behalf of Westminster City Council and Society of London Theatre).

Underbelly recently partnered with Wessex Grove to produce the critically acclaimed production of *Macbeth* starring Ralph Fiennes and Indira Varma, as it toured to Liverpool (The Depot), Edinburgh (Royal Highland Centre), London (Dock X) and Washington DC (Shakespeare Theatre Company).

Other credits include The McOnie Company's *Nutcracker* at the Tuff Nutt Jazz Club (Southbank Centre), *Tweedy's Massive Circus* (UK Tour), *Five Guys Named Moe* (Marble Arch Theatre) Oliver Award-nominated for Best Entertainment; *Cabaret Royale* (Gaillard Centre, Charleston USA); and *La Clique* (London, Manchester and Singapore 2021).

www.underbelly.co.uk | @FollowTheCow | @underbellyedinburgh

Underbelly

Directors	Ed Bartlam and Charlie Wood
PA to Directors and Office Manager	Lauren Manning
Head of Programming and Producer	Marina Dixon
Senior Programmer	Aisling Galligan
Senior Producer	Áine Flanagan
Programme Coordinator	Alex Cofield
Head of Marketing	Lauren Carroll
Marketing Manager	Demi McAleer
Marketing Executive	Hope Martin
Social Media and Content Officer	Angus Livingstone
Head of Production	Ian Gibbs
Production Manager	Kenny Easson
Technical Manager	Andrew Gorman
Warehouse and Logistics Manager	Steven Kilpatrick
Production Coordinator	Joe Ewing
Senior Event Producer	Ruth Fisher
Event Producer	Rachel Sivills-McCann
Executive Producer	Holly Reiss
Head of Operations	Ryan Beattie
Operations Manager	Joe Mills
Head of Ticketing	Natalie Norman
Head of Bars	Jonny Brown
Head of Brand Partnerships	Mary Gleeson
Head of Finance	Jace Subramoney

UNTAPPED

UNDERBELLY | NEW DIORAMA THEATRE | CONCORD THEATRICALS

Originally developed in 2018 by New Diorama and Underbelly to discover and support emerging theatre makers at the Edinburgh Festival Fringe, the Untapped Award has established a remarkable record as a platform for bold new theatre by outstanding companies.

Over the last six years, the Untapped Award has provided a springboard for a diverse array of major Edinburgh Fringe premieres. Previous recipients have gone on to win three Fringe First Awards – *This is Not a Show About Hong Kong* (Max Percy & Friends); *It's True, It's True, It's True* (Breach); *Dressed* (ThisEgg) – and *The Stage* Edinburgh Award – *Queens of Sheba* (Nouveau Riche). Winners have also gone on to secure major national and international tours following the festival, including Side eYe Productions' *Dugsi Dayz* (Royal Court transfer), FlawBored's *It's A Motherf**king Pleasure* (*The Stage*'s The Fringe Five), Burnt Lemon's *Tokyo Rose*, Ugly Bucket's *Good Grief* and Nouveau Riche's *Queens of Sheba*, which most recently played at New York's Public Theater for the prestigious Under the Radar Festival; and adaptations for screen, with *It's True, It's True, It's True* broadcast on BBC television.

"The Untapped trio ranked among the best of the entire festival, proof that support from organisations like Underbelly and New Diorama can pay off in spades." – *WhatsOnStage*

In 2023, the award was relaunched and super-charged with support from new partner Concord Theatricals, with the cash investment in each company doubled to £10,000 alongside an extensive paid-for support package and publication by Concord Theatricals under their UK imprint Samuel French Ltd.

Drawn from a nationwide talent search, the three 2024 winners are *Ugly Sisters* by piss / CARNATION, an operatic, heretic and parasitic dissection of Germaine Greer, sisterhood and all feminist history; *The Mosinee Project* by Counterfactual, a fevered, darkly funny retelling of a true story about a fake Communist invasion in a small American town; and *DRUM* by Our Day, a joyful and poignant play capturing a unique snapshot of London's Ghanaian diaspora in the swinging sixties.

COUNTERFACTUAL

Counterfactual is a theatre and performance company. We make shows that tap into the strange, complicated underbelly of contemporary life, investigating how the past and our memory of it brought us here. Created and led by Artistic Director Nikhil Vyas (*Dismissed*, Soho Theatre, *My Life As A Cowboy*, Park Theatre), Counterfactual pieces together collaborations across different disciplines, informed by the needs of the story at hand. *The Mosinee Project* is the company's debut full production.

CAST

JONATHAN OLDFIELD
John Decker/Mayor Ralph E Kronenwetter

Jonathan Oldfield is an actor, writer and director. He trained at the Bristol Old Vic Theatre School.

As an actor, his credits include *The Power* (Amazon Prime), *Romeo and Juliet* (USA tour), *Petal* (Omnibus Theatre), *Twelfth Night* (Kew Gardens), *Nicholas Nickleby* (Bristol Old Vic).

As a writer, he is co-creator of BBC Radio 4 comedy series *Time of the Week* starring Sian Clifford, and his storytelling show *One Way Mirror* was winner of the Brighton Fringe Trapeze Media Bursary 2024.

As a director, his credits include the multi-award-winning *Lorna Rose Treen: Skin Pigeon* which was named third best comedy show of 2023 in *The Telegraph* and *Joe Kent Walters is Frankie Monroe: Live!!!* which was the winner of Best Show at Leicester Comedy Festival 2024. He is a Pleasance Theatre Associate Artist 2024–26.

MARTHA WATSON ALLPRESS
Benjamin Gitlow/Francis Schweinler

Martha Watson Allpress is an actor and writer from the East Midlands.

Acting credits include: *The Beautiful Future is Coming* (Jermyn Street Theatre), *I Know I Know I Know* (Southwark Playhouse), *All One Fabric* (The Yard Theatre), *My Mad Fat Diary* (Channel 4), *Spectrum* (Bark Films).

Writing credits include: *Lady Dealer* (Bush Theatre), *The Christmas That Got Forgot* (HMP Spring Hill and Kestrel), *Kick* (Lyric Hammersmith), *Patricia Gets Ready* (national tour). She also has multiple screen projects in development with production companies such as VAL and Red Planet Pictures.

MILLICENT WONG
Joseph Zack Kornfeder

Theatre credits include: *The Crucible* (Sheffield Crucible); *Sputnik Sweetheart* (Arcola Theatre); *Orlando* (Garrick Theatre); *Henry V* (Donmar Warehouse); *Athena* (The Yard Theatre); *After Life* (National Theatre); *The Doctor* (Duke of York's Theatre); *The Lion, the Witch and the Wardrobe* (The Bridge Theatre); *The King of Hell's Palace* (Hampstead Theatre); *Pah-La* (Royal Court Theatre); *Six Degrees of Separation, Macbeth, Richard III, A Streetcar Named Desire, A View From the Bridge, As You Like It, Closer, Three Sisters* (Royal Central School of Speech and Drama); *Forbidden City: Portrait of an Empress* (Singapore Repertory Theatre); *Beauty World* (Victoria Theatre, Singapore).

Television credits include: *Douglas is Cancelled* (ITV); *Dal Y Mellt* (Vox Pictures); *Silent Witness, Dracula* (BBC); *Annika* (Alibi / UKTV).

Film credits include: *I Used to Be Famous*.

CREATIVE

NIKHIL VYAS | Writer/Director

Nikhil Vyas is a theatre director & maker, born in Mumbai and raised in Croydon, whose practice includes dramaturgy, education & participatory work. He trained at Bristol Old Vic Theatre School and the Young Vic Directors Program. His credits as director or lead artist include *Dismissed* (Soho Theatre), *Haunting & Renting* (Five Shorts, Young Vic), *My Life As A Cowboy* (Park Theatre), *Dances For PowerPoint* (Siobhan Davies Dance), *Progress* (Camden People's Theatre/ZOO Venues Edinburgh), *How My Light Is Spent* (Wardrobe Theatre).

His credits as assistant director include *Bhangra Nation* (Birmingham Repertory Theatre), *Chasing Hares* (Young Vic), *'Night Mother* (Hampstead Theatre), *Civilisation* (New Diorama Theatre), *Wild Goose Dreams* (Theatre Royal Bath).

AARON KILERCIOGLU | Original Co-Creator/Dramaturg

Raised in Vienna by Turkish-Canadian parents, Aaron is a writer and director based in London. This blend of cultures illustrates his ability to translate between English, German, and Turkish. Currently, he is writing a feature film for Karga7 Pictures, an original play commission for Eleanor Lloyd Productions, and a musical adaptation of a TV series for PSM Istanbul.

His most recent play *The EU Killed My Dad* was staged at the Jermyn Street Theatre in January of this year and won the Woven Voices Prize as well as receiving two Offie nominations. His previous play, *For a Palestinian*, enjoyed a sell-out three week run at the Camden People's Theatre, before transferring to, and selling out, the Bristol Old Vic Theatre. Both are published with Methuen Drama.

His previous work has been shortlisted for the Theatre503 International Playwriting Prize, and won the BOLD Playwrights Prize as well as the Methuen Drama 'Other' Prize. Aaron has been a member of numerous associations and groups including, Old Vic Playwriting, Bush Theatre Emerging Writers, Royal Court Young Agitators, and London Library Emerging Writers.

His short films have been screened at festivals across the globe.

GRACE VENNING | Set & Costume Designer

Grace trained at the Royal Welsh College of Music and Drama. She was a resident design assistant at the National Theatre in 2018–19.

Design credits include: *Titus Andronicus* (Shakespeare's Globe), *If Not Now, When* (National Theatre), *The Maladies* (Almeida Theatre), *Antonio e Cleopatra* (Buxton International Festival), *Everyday* (New Diorama and Deafinitely Theatre), *Before I Was a Bear* (Soho Theatre), *Svadba* (Waterperry Opera Festival), *The Importance of Being Earnest* (RADA), *I Stand For What I Stand On* (Strike A Light), *Back Into the World* (English Touring Opera: associate designer), *Let the Right One In* (LAMDA), *You Stupid Darkness!* (Southwark Playhouse: associate designer), *Penny* (Pleasance), *Time of Listening* (Snape Maltings), Opera Scenes (Guildhall School of Music and Drama), *La bohème* (Clonter Opera), *Semele* (Mid Wales Opera tour), *i will still be whole [...]*; *FCUK'D* (Bunker), *The Death of Ivan Ilyich* (Attic Theatre Co.), *My Life as a Cowboy* (Park Theatre), *In My Lungs [...]* (VAULT Festival).

CATJA HAMILTON | Lighting Designer

Catja is a Lighting Designer and Co-Director of Airlock Theatre. She is a former Creative Associate at Jermyn Street Theatre and Resident Designer at NDT Broadgate. Her previous credits include: *Talawa Firsts on Tour* (Talawa Studio & UK tour), *Pansexual Pregnant Piracy* (Soho Theatre), *Scarlet Sunday* (Omnibus Theatre), *The Pursuit of Joy* (Jermyn Street Theatre), *The Wolf, The Duck, and The Mouse* (Unicorn Theatre), *Passing* (Park Theatre), *Rip Van Winkle* (Hoxton Hall), *The Importance of Being... Earnest?* (UK tour), *Sorry We Didn't Die At Sea* (Park Theatre), *Birthright* (Finborough Theatre), *Agrippina* (Jackson's Lane), *The Oyster Problem* (Jermyn Street Theatre), *SNAIL* (VAULT Festival), *Acid's Reign* (VAULT Festival), *Lesbian Space Crime* (Soho Theatre), *Cassandra* (UK tour), *Time and Tide* (UK tour), *Another America* (Park Theatre), *Paradise Lost* (The Shipwright), *The Anarchist* (Jermyn Street Theatre), *An Intervention* (Riverside Studios), *Lizard King* (UK tour), *The 4th Country* (Park Theatre).

PATCH MIDDLETON | Sound Designer

Patch Middleton is a composer and sound designer from Cumbria now based in Manchester. His work often explores the strange and fantastical, from conjuring ghost stories inside an abandoned mansion to creating soundscapes for a cowboy-noir fever dream set in the Nevada desert. He is fascinated by the blurred lines between reality and story, and between music and noise. Recent projects include: *Ghosts of the Near Future* (Summerhall, August 2022 & Barbican, October 2023), *soundlandscape* (Theatre by the Lake, October 2021, & Ilkley Literature Festival, July to October 2023), and *The Mosinee Project* (Underbelly, August 2024).

DAN LIGHT | Video System Designer

Dan Light is a video designer based in London, working in the UK and internationally. He graduated from the Guildhall School of Music and Drama in 2022, receiving the Lord Mayor's Prize.

In addition to working on national tours, new musicals, and large-scale events, Dan has an established presence in the West End, with productions including *Instructions For a Teenage Armageddon* (Garrick Theatre), concert performances of *For Tonight* (Adelphi Theatre) and *Bat Boy: The Musical* (London Palladium), and the English-language premiere of *Your Lie In April* (Harold Pinter Theatre).

Dan regularly collaborates with FRAY Studios as an Associate Video Designer to Finn Ross on their portfolio of productions and events, notably Vogue World London, a theatre-inspired fashion show broadcast from Theatre Royal Drury Lane. As Associate Video Designer to David Bergman, Dan worked on the West End transfer of Sydney Theatre Company's award-winning production of *The Picture of Dorian Gray* starring Sarah Snook, which was praised for its innovative use of video design.

JESSIE ANAND | Producer

Jessie is a freelance producer working across theatre and opera. Credits include: *The Bleeding Tree* and *Yellowfin* (Southwark Playhouse), *Pansexual Pregnant Piracy* (Soho Theatre), *This Might Not Be It* (Bush Theatre), *Antisemitism: a (((musical)))* (Camden People's Theatre), *The Silly Little Mouse* (Bold Tendencies), *Orlando* (59E59, New York/Pleasance, Edinburgh Fringe/VAULT Festival), *Pennyroyal* (Finborough Theatre), *Cabildo* (Arcola Theatre/Wilton's Music Hall) and *Blue Thunder* (VAULT Festival). She has also worked with and for companies including the National Theatre, Belarus Free Theatre, Wayward Productions and Kandinsky. Jessie's productions have been nominated for multiple Offies and she is supported by new producers' charity Stage One.

CHARACTERS

Primarily:
JOSEPH ZACK KORNFEDER
BENJAMIN GITLOW
JOHN DECKER
FRANCIS SCHWEINLER
MAYOR RALPH E KRONENWETTER

More variously:
The **TOWNSPEOPLE** of Mosinee, Wisconsin
The **PRESS** of the United States of America
US, here and now

SETTING

Mosinee, Wisconsin, United States of America.
Wherever else we might be.

TIME

Late January–Early May, 1950
Some time after then.

AUTHOR'S NOTES

As a director who is often exasperated by the sight of stage directions, I feel duty bound to relieve any would-be interpreters of this play of any burden in what any of the following should look like. When I made this play, I made a number of decisions in organising people, objects, sounds, space, time, and feelings, that were organic to the specific conditions of the process we found ourselves in. For example, we had three performers, some set design, some lights, and some cameras and videos. Two pieces of music featured prominently – Alban Berg's *Violin Concerto*, as performed by the Berlin Philharmonic Orchestra, and Fleetwood Mac's 'Don't Stop'. I am very happy with the decisions I made in that process of organisation, but by no means expect anyone else to make even remotely similar ones.

If you're reading this, you probably also already know what the business of dots and dashes in a playtext means. All text in *italics* indicates a moment when performers – as themselves, in any number or combination – talk to an audience, in the year of when a performance takes place. All text in *(italics and brackets)* indicates performance that was created live by the company. All spaces between lines indicate rhythm.

The Mosinee Project, at its heart, is a speculation on a real event, real people, real places, real things, and I would offer that you should take up that speculation on your own terms.

Have fun. Good luck.

ACKNOWLEDGEMENTS

They say it takes a village to raise a play – in the ruthlessly denuded landscape of the contemporary arts, this feels truer than ever. *The Mosinee Project* has been a process of intense scrimping and from the first R&D onwards, and there are many hands who helped me with raising.

Thanks to:
Gabi Spiro
Blythe Brett
Beth Drury
Breffni Holahan
Jessica Layde
who all helped me with the first flights.

Stella Green
James Nash
Rohan Perumatantri
Ash Gupta
Emma Clark
Emma Jude Harris
Jaz Woodcock-Stewart
Robin Hellier
for insight, expertise and encouragement.

Brian Logan and the team at CPT
Sheila and the team at Talawa
Rose and the team at Turf Arts
Bec and the team at NDT
Alex and the team at Underbelly
Pierre and the team at Centre 151
Hattie and the team at Siobhan Davies Studios
Daniel and the team at MGCFutures
The Unity Theatre Trust
Arts Council England
Multitude Media
Cup Of Ambition
Guy J Sanders
for space, support, means and materiel.

Martha
Millie
Jon
for soul, imagination and humour.

Grace, Patch, Catja, Dan, Josh
for patience, skill and nerve.

Jessie
for everything.

Aaron
for everything, from the beginning.

Mum and Dad
always.

Dedicated to Emily, my peace.

ACT ONE

DECKER. Well, truth be told, whatever explanation I give you, it'll all seem a little far-fetched now, but...none of you can imagine what that time was like. What we... were facing. We had to act. Had to do something. And it began with me hearing that speech, Joe McCarthy's speech.

What made the most impression on me later, was the piece of paper. How he held it aloft in his hand, like this. It didn't even occur to me that it was a prop. It just seemed to say, this problem is not in your head. It is real. So real you can hold it in your hand.

And the number he gave, 57. It...felt precise. Not a number plucked out of thin air.

He just held this piece of paper in his hand, with those 57 communists on it, and the implication was, he could crush it, whenever he felt like it. And perhaps, crush them, whenever he felt like it.

As I left that speech, the whole journey home my mind was racing. It felt like something was activated in me. I'd known about Commies before this, of course, you know, Alger Hiss, Liz Bentley, the rest of them – and, of course, the Legion, it was all anyone would talk about. But as I was travelling home, I felt like I was seeing everything different. That's the funny thing about a speech like that, what it does to the imagination.

I thought I could see them everywhere. Commies, I mean. Thought I saw one loitering outside the drugstore. Thought I saw one, sweeping the street near my car. Thought I saw one, next to the streetlight by my porch.

DECKER. Got me thinking, that's how you tell a story. Don't give the whole game away. Let the audience imagine. Much more effective.

And that was how it started. Must all seem a little far-fetched now, but…none of you can imagine what that time was like. What we…were facing. We had to act. And at that moment, certainly I didn't think it would end in…anybody dying.

SCHWEINLER. Of course I was enthusiastic! Listen, Mosinee's the most honest, hard-working, god-fearing community in the country. So long as Mosinee's been on the map, there's been a Schweinler there. We helped put it on the map! So when John Decker pitched it one of our state Legion meetings: some kind of…demonstration of life under Commie rule, in a local town, I immediately replied, sign us up! Us, being Mosinee. The most honest, hard-working god-fearing community in the United States. Being as I am the editor of the *Mosinee Times*, I knew my people well. Knew this'd be a…shot in the arm for them. And that I could probably get some sponsorship from Preston's Quality Bakery in the bag too.

So I started to get the ball rolling, discussing it with the Mayor. But next thing I know…

DECKER. An educational experience. That was the plan, at first. For the youngsters, maybe? But pretty soon I realised we needed some expertise. You know, here we were trying to create an educational experience about this problem, but what the heck do I know about being a Red? And I didn't exactly have a rolodex of communists I could call up and ask them, 'what is it you believe in and how do you go about trying to achieve it?'

So I made some enquiries at the Legion, and, within, I don't know, a couple of weeks, he appeared.

*

KORNFEDER. Flyers? Flags? A marching band? I don't see a lot of progress here.

DECKER. From as soon as he arrived, he cut to the chase, no pleasantries. I would discover that was his preferred method of communication. He went straight over to my steno pad and started rifling through, and I tried to explain we'd only really gotten the ball rolling, and that, you know, this was for a local audience, so we had to cater to those...tastes...

KORNFEDER. What do you imagine when I say to you, Communism?

SCHWEINLER. Now, when you serve in the military, as I have, you get used to all manner of Tom, Dick and Harry trying to impress you with some newfangled idea. You get used to dealing with it in an efficient manner. So I told him, well, look, I mean, it's not any damn way I want to live. Told him, I like my liberty, as written in the Constitution, which they don't have. Told him, I like being on the side of progress, which they don't have. And I told him I like the feeling of safety and security, which they don't have. To which, he replied –

KORNFEDER. You feel safe?

SCHWEINLER. Well, yes.

KORNFEDER. Well, then why would you be planning something like this?

SCHWEINLER. I didn't appreciate that.

DECKER. I tried my best to turn the question on him, and to ask him, well, what was his impression of the Commies? Because, after all, he was the expert who'd been sent, so clearly, he should know. To which he only replied –

KORNFEDER. With respect to you both, gentlemen, you seem to be shying away from what is at stake here. Flags and marching bands and singing 'God Bless

America' are all well enough for the annual state fair, but what you're proposing to deal with – Communism – is alarming, and if you want people to learn, you have to alarm them. You don't achieve that with a lecture, or presentation, or pageant. You have to make something that will happen live. To make people feel something. To feel fear. And that is something that can only happen in bodies, in the right time, in the right space, in the right conditions. Have I described it accurately?

DECKER. Yes, sir.

SCHWEINLER. Yes.

KORNFEDER. You are on the cusp of something that could transform the political life of the nation. You have the right time. You have the right space. Now I'm going to help you to create the right conditions.

DECKER. And then he gave us a suggestion for the day this would happen on – 1st May 1950.

SCHWEINLER. I remember coming away from that, thinking, who the hell have I got myself mixed up with? Got in my car, drove to straight to Wausau to find some answers. I went to the *Herald* building, into the back room where they keep their archives, started digging back through the clippings and –

Joseph Zack Kornfeder. There was a file on him.

Moved here from Slovakia in 1915. Joined the Communist Party in 1919, as a garment worker. Started as an organizer in Harlem, then joined the district committee, then became district organiser, then labor unions activities secretary, then joined the top rank of the national committee. Moved to Moscow for three years. Joined the Lenin School. Trained in underground political warfare. Moved to Columbia and Venezuela as part of the Communist International.

And then, in 1934, he just...left. Left the Party. Turned his back on it all. This Kornfeder, he'd been as Red as you get, until one day, he just decided, magically, that he wasn't.

And this was the man we were handing over Mosinee, the most honest, god-fearing town in the USA to?

*

Good afternoon. Thank you for joining us. It's nice to see you all. I'm aware there's quite a lot that's been thrown at you, so I just wanted to check in, explain where I'm at currently.

I think it's probably best to start with...America. In case you didn't guess, that's where all this is happening.

How do you imagine America?

Maybe baseball? Eagles? Apple pies? Stadiums? White picket fences? Those really big houses, which spread out over way wider patches of ground than we get over here? Guns? Racism? Trump?

I find it impossible to imagine America. It feels too vast to pin down. I can't get my head around it. There's just too many things within America to comprehend. All the way back to when we studied it in school, I would be told this thing and that about the place, and I couldn't figure out how to piece it together. I've only really been to New York City, and that pretty much was beyond the limits of my imagination.

And yet I started to think of America, a little bit, like a parent. Or guardian, at least. Do you know what I mean? It's not always a very nice parent. Or a very fair one. But you know how, as a child, when you see your parent is ill, or really upset, it affects you really, really deeply? Like it's as if you're feeling ill, or upset, vicariously through them?

I still feel that way about America today. When America is unwell, it makes me feel a little unwell. Or when America is in danger over something, I feel like I'm in danger, or as if the worst might come to pass. Like, when America is erupting over a problem, then that problem must be at its worst possible version imaginable. I start to feel afraid that whatever that problem is in the world, it very soon will engulf us all here. I feel all this much more personally than I would expect of someone of my... politics.

When we started researching the events at Mosinee in 1950, I found John Decker and Francis Schweinler's interviews, about this man, Joseph Zack Kornfeder and we'd found my way in, to understanding it. Because Joseph Zack Kornfeder was an outsider, but one whose job it was to help Americans imagine themselves better. In higher definition. An expert in imagination. We realised, through his eyes, we could maybe start to imagine the whole country in better detail.

So now let's picture Kornfeder.

Let's assume you've imagined a man. Let's assume you've imagined a white man. This is 1950, so you're probably on the money. What else are you imagining?

Is he the big bad wolf? Or is he Robin Hood?

A real former Communist, revisiting his former identity to make the Day Under Communism feel more real, this is whose steps we've tried to retrace.

ACT TWO

KORNFEDER. Describe it to me. A day in the life of this town.

DECKER. Any...particular day of the week?

KORNFEDER. What day will it be? On the day?

DECKER. So, a Monday, so...

SCHWEINLER. Well, I'd go in to work.

KORNFEDER. Which is where?

SCHWEINLER. The *Mosinee Times* office.

KORNFEDER. What route would you take?

SCHWEINLER. Erm...via Western Avenue.

KORNFEDER. Give me more detail.

SCHWEINLER. Well, I'd... I live over here. At the Southeast suburb. So I drive in over the bridge going from...east to west. And then that leads down past Drengler's Tavern and Preston's Quality Bakery.

KORNFEDER. And what time is it?

SCHWEINLER. 6.30 a.m.

KORNFEDER. So you'd see the dawn?

SCHWEINLER. I...suppose I do. But I don't pay too much attention at that time. I'm just thinking about work. And the day ahead.

KORNFEDER. And you get yourself something nice at the bakery? Something to prepare you for the day ahead?

SCHWEINLER. Well, usually my wife has made breakfast, so... Maybe I'd stop there for a coffee, at least.

Why is that relevant?

KORNFEDER. And what else is happening around town, in the morning.

DECKER. So, lots of folk would be going to Church, or coming back, depending what time you mean...

KORNFEDER. Where are the churches?

DECKER. Lutheran church here, Baptist church there. And Catholic's there...but I should say now, sir, that the Catholic church, they aren't interested in being involved in whatever it is that you're...that we're planning.

But I can get back to them, and maybe they'll change their mind – in fact, let me get back to them. I'll get back to them today.

KORNFEDER. Where else would people be going? On this fine Monday morning?

DECKER. So, yes, so, Church, and then folk usually head into town to work. The Paper Mill in particular.

KORNFEDER. Is that the main employer?

SCHWEINLER. That's right.

KORNFEDER. Tell me more about the place. What do people do.

SCHWEINLER. I really don't know what you're after, sir. It's an ordinary town of two thousand people.

DECKER. Well, if you're interested in knowing the options for recreation, fishing's very popular, I believe. The Mayor's quite fond of it, I'm told. And then there's a movie theatre, and then...and then...there's shopping along this edge of the lake...but if you want anything more extravagant, then usually folk go Milwaukee ways.

KORNFEDER. And how do you end your Monday in this ordinary town? Mr Decker?

DECKER. Well, I don't really live there, I'm from Milwaukee. So I probably just go back there. But, um, on the occasion, I do to stay in town, I usually go bowling.

Over, um, here.

At the bowling alley.

KORNFEDER. Mr Schweinler?

SCHWEINLER. Well. My preferred way to end the day is at my home, sir. With my wife, Irene. There isn't anything more pleasant in the whole world, then to go back after a hard day's work, have her take my jacket, fix me a bourbon and serve me a piping hot dinner.

I'm sorry if you were after something more…extravagant.

KORNFEDER. No, that's quite perfect, Mr Schweinler. Where are the weak spots in Mosinee?

SCHWEINLER. What do you mean?

KORNFEDER. Pressure points. Nodes of instability, we called it at the Academy. Zones where there is a critical mass of potentiality for social disruption. That's where a movement can be catalysed.

DECKER. That's, uh, well, I think Francis is probably better placed to say than I am, but, uh,

SCHWEINLER. There isn't anything like that in this town.

KORNFEDER. You have to look at where in the town the most potent aggregation of complaint may lie. And that is where our Day Under Communism begins.

The Paper Mill. Are the workers there unionised?

SCHWEINLER. They are in the process of it, but it's, uh, it's complicated…

KORNFEDER. In the process…but not complete?

SCHWEINLER. Correct.

KORNFEDER. All the better. This Mill will be where the day begins.

DECKER. Come again?

KORNFEDER. Step by step over the course of the day, a conflagration spreads from a wildcat strike at the Paper Mill, which triggers a mass proletarian uprising, culminating in a coup d'etat, and the execution of the Mayor.

DECKER. What?

KORNFEDER. You need a violent decapitation of the power structure.

This is, by the way, the textbook case of what we studied at the Academy.

*

Now, unlike John Decker or Francis Schweinler or the other planners, Kornfeder never gave any interviews after the fact, to explain his experience. In fact, there are only scraps of material remaining from his own hand that shed light on what he was thinking. Here's what we found from one of his remaining journals, a couple of days after his arrival:

KORNFEDER. As I walked into the town, I took a route through their commercial quarter. Adverts everywhere. Even in a town this small, one cannot escape the neon. Shopfronts draped with coats and gloves and refrigerators and bathtubs and microwave ovens. Salesmen offering me new shoes or Cadillacs or record players. I kept my head down and walked by.

Even now, at the end of the day, I watched the people amiably making their way through shops and markets, chattering and laughing gaily. It was as if the world was passing them by. Like the times as I was experiencing them did not really exist. I realised that the whole town, really, was behind a store-front, sitting idly for passer-bys to ogle at, inattentive to the burglars in their midst, and I was gripped by a feeling of wanting to smash through the window, and sound the alarms, and scream at them, 'do you know what is at stake here? Do you know the size of the problem we're facing?'

Mr Decker and Mr Schweinler expect my return tomorrow. I know now that these people will need encouragement to see their world they way I do.

*

Are there any questions? About the nature of the task? Good. When you're ready, Mr Schweinler.

SCHWEINLER. Darling, I'm home.

DECKER. Oh, how wonderful, honey. Let me take your coat.

SCHWEINLER. Oh, uh, thank you.

DECKER. What about a drink? Can I fix you a bourbon?

SCHWEINLER. I think…maybe…

DECKER. I've made your favourite, tonight, meatloaf. I really wanted to treat you.

SCHWEINLER. Can we, can we stop?

KORNFEDER. What's wrong?

SCHWEINLER. I'm finding it a little, uh, difficult.

KORNFEDER. Maybe…think about the way you would enter the house, in this situation.

SCHWEINLER. As myself?

KORNFEDER. As a Communist would.

SCHWEINLER. But I'm undercover.

KORNFEDER. No. There's a difference. You're trying to stay undercover. It will reveal itself in the way it should. Just focus on the task.

SCHWEINLER. Irene, I'm home.

DECKER. Oh, darling, I'm glad. Let me take your –

SCHWEINLER. I don't think you need to, I can do it.

DECKER. Oh, well, OK –

KORNFEDER. Good.

DECKER. Let me do that, honey.

SCHWEINLER. No, I can get my own drink...

DECKER. Please, honey, I'd be happy to.

KORNFEDER. And what drink is that, Irene?

DECKER. Bourbon.

SCHWEINLER. Irene, bourbon, on a Monday night... I think we're fine with water, aren't we?

DECKER. But, but...I just want to help you relax?

SCHWEINLER. No trouble on that front, I think I'm very relaxed, aren't you? Can I get you a water, too?

DECKER. ...Fine.

SCHWEINLER. It's good to, to, treat each other as equals, isn't it? There you go.

DECKER. Honey, can we talk?

SCHWEINLER. Of course.

DECKER. Look, I've made meatloaf for us tonight, which I know is your favourite...

SCHWEINLER. But that's so much hard work for you...

DECKER. But I just... I want to look after you.

KORNFEDER. Isn't it excessive?

SCHWEINLER. Look, darling, it's unnecessary. I'm very, uh, happy with uh...frivolities like that, I don't think...

DECKER. Honey, what's going on?

SCHWEINLER. I'm concerned, Irene, that our household is losing its moral structure. We have each other. We don't need to burden ourselves with all the...ornamentation, especially now, as our nation is...

DECKER. I went to the store today, and I bought you some new gloves, honey. Would you like to see them?

KORNFEDER. Go get them.

SCHWEINLER. Irene, that's very good of you, but...we don't... did you keep the receipt?

DECKER. Here.

SCHWEINLER. Irene, I have gloves.

DECKER. But they're old. And worn out. I just think you deserve it. And it's so cold out...

SCHWEINLER. Exactly, so wouldn't you say it's money that could be better spent on those who need it? To supply them with gloves and coats?

DECKER. But I... you need new gloves.

SCHWEINLER. I have gloves.

DECKER. But you need new ones.

SCHWEINLER. Why?

DECKER. Because...

I'm sorry, I'm finding this –

KORNFEDER. Stay in it.

DECKER. Because I just wanted to do a nice thing for you and get you new gloves.

SCHWEINLER. And I don't care about nice things. Nice things aren't important. I care about the community, and I want you to start caring about them too.

DECKER. Well, what do you want me to go out and buy gloves for fucking everybody?

SCHWEINLER. What would be so wrong with that? Every housewife on this darn street has probably gone and bought a new pair of gloves, or a scarf, or a coat today, and meanwhile the men at the Mill are freezing, so badly, to the point where their fingers are turning black. And they have to go back, again and again, day after day. And I have to go past them, on my way to work tomorrow, wearing my fancy new gloves?

DECKER. Well, that's hardly fair as a comparison, because some people work harder than others, you work your ass off every day...

SCHWEINLER. Do you think I work harder than you?

DECKER. Yes!

SCHWEINLER. You, who holds down our home, raise our children,

DECKER. You go out all day and put food on our table, I couldn't do that –

SCHWEINLER. Are you serious? Irene, where is your ambition?

What ambition have you ever had in your life? For yourself? For society?

DECKER. I have tried my hardest. And I will continue to try my hardest, to be your wife. Because I love you.

SCHWEINLER. And I've just articulated that there is more to life than that.

KORNFEDER. Good work, gentlemen. Let's stop this there. Let's have some thoughts on what that was like.

DECKER. Okay, well, I don't know what the fuck that was. What were you saying?

SCHWEINLER. I was doing what I was told to do. What about you? With your faffing about?

DECKER. What do you mean?

SCHWEINLER. Your faffing. Your stuttering. The way you couldn't articulate a thought, the way you refused, blindly, to deviate from a single train of thought? It was so shallow, so infuriating, so vapid, Irene – I mean, Decker,

KORNFEDER. I think we take the point.

SCHWEINLER. We don't have any children. I mentioned she raises our children – we don't have any.

KORNFEDER. I hope this demonstration was clear to you both. How Communism begins in the home.

If we want to teach the people of Mosinee, this is the logic we need to reveal. And to embody.

*

In the last week of March, Kornfeder submitted his plans to the American Legion HQ:

KORNFEDER. Gentlemen, I write with enthusiasm and confidence in the progress being made at Mosinee these past weeks. The citizens of this town will awaken on May first to challenge and introspect on their sacred duty as democratic agents in the face of Communist subversion. Already they are being trained to be alert to the threats within the fabric of their domestic order. With your continued trust and support, this process will be a transformative intervention. Enclosed is a full timetable for the day.

Instead of trust and support, what came back a week later was:

GITLOW. Well, old friend, it's been so many years!

KORNFEDER. What do you mean, Mr Schweinler?

GITLOW. Schweinler? It's Benjamin Gitlow, Zack. Is everything OK?

Ben Gitlow and Kornfeder were similar. Both were outsiders. His parents were Russian Jews who'd fled to the US before the Revolution. He'd been at the founding of the American Communist Party in 1919. He'd spent the next decade fighting for the movement. He'd turned his back on the Party in 1934. You'd think they'd be pals.

But, from Kornfeder's journal...

KORNFEDER. What gives that little bastard the right to trample over what is rightfully mine he hasn't been to moscow he doesn't know what i know the little shitheel should be busy peddling his stupid little books to his fans and to the fucking new york times and go on his fucking lecture circuits and speaking tours and leave the actual hard work of politics to the rest of us.

I'm surprised to see you here. Is it as part of the program? What are you doing to my maps?

GITLOW. I've just arrived here today, Zack. On behalf of Legion HQ.

KORNFEDER. I see. Well, it was my skills that they'd asked for towards this assignment, so, I don't know what more you'd be offering? Too many ex-communists spoil the broth.

GITLOW. What is it you're trying to achieve here, Zack?

Coup d'etats. Union turbulence. Fifth columnists plotting in these nice little houses.

KORNFEDER. Look, I just think...

GITLOW. Break-ins of churches. Execution of the Mayor. You know this is supposed to be fiction, right?

KORNFEDER. What is the point of conceiving of an event like this, if you don't follow it through to its endpoint?

These people around here are sleeping. There's nothing behind their eyes. They don't know what we know. We have a, a, a, responsibility to show them how susceptible they are.

GITLOW. They are?

KORNFEDER. I mean, we are.

GITLOW. I hear the date was your idea. May 1st.

KORNFEDER. I suggested it, yes.

GITLOW. International Worker's Day. Christmas for the Commies. Do you remember how we'd celebrate? In the Bronx.

KORNFEDER. That was all a long time ago.

GITLOW. Do you remember the speeches you would make? It was like seeing Lenin himself, in the flesh.

You're an intellectual, Zack. You always did like big ideas. And I understand the appeal of all this. You can pull out your old volumes of *Capital*. Your old textbooks from Moscow. Maybe, on the day of this coup, you can do some lessons on the value form for teenagers at the High School.

KORNFEDER. Don't patronise me, Ben. You know what's been taken from me.

GITLOW. Yes, of course. Nadezdha and Leon. One can only imagine.

But you know, this only adds to the Legion's question of your…temperament.

KORNFEDER. What?

GITLOW. Whether you're the right person to lead this operation. Because you know what this all sounds like, to an outsider.

KORNFEDER. Enlighten me.

GITLOW. Like you're still Red. Like you want it to happen, but real.

KORNFEDER. I,

Why would I want that?

GITLOW. You tell me.

KORNFEDER. I can't quite –

Is that what you've been telling them?

GITLOW. Me? No.

Look, I'm not the villain here, Zack. I understand your perspective.

We both know what these people – these Americans – are like. In their little towns, with their little aspirations and their little disappointments.

They like a story, and the simpler the better.

So we should play their game, and give them that.

*

> (**JOHN DECKER** *is imagining a town in the USSR. After about two minutes of this –*)

Thank you, Mr Decker.

Quite a vision for us to be working towards, gentlemen?

KORNFEDER. I mean, that isn't what it's like, at all. I've actually been in the Soviet Union. If you want to know what one of those towns is actually like –

GITLOW. It isn't one of your towns we want to know about right now, Zack. It's theirs.

*

KORNFEDER. Since then, Gitlow has begun to dismantle what I was building, brick by brick, day by day.

GITLOW. There's a feeling at Legion HQ about what this town needs for this day, what America needs for this day to be, is a little bit...brassier than what you've pitched.

KORNFEDER. April 3rd. The decision has been made that my plan is too inconvenient. Too subtle.

GITLOW. You're the expert in the Soviet Communistic experience, Zack. Isn't that right? And that's perfect, for a Soviet invasion of the town.

KORNFEDER. They didn't like my idea for it to be based on an internal threat. They didn't think that there was a risk of subversion within Mosinee. Apparently, for them, that was beyond the pale.

GITLOW. So there will be barricades going up across Baring Street, and Green Street and Western Avenue. And they will be manned by soldiers, dressed as Soviets, and those soldiers will come from out of town. When Mosineeans wake up, they will wake up to something external, something unrecognisable, something foreign.

KORNFEDER. And the lesson from that is?

GITLOW. How to resist an invader.

KORNFEDER. But, this, this just undermines everything that could be interesting and radical about this project –

GITLOW. *Radical?*

KORNFEDER. April 6th. What could be radical is becoming a charade. Roles have been assigned to us. Gitlow is to be 'General Secretary'. I am to be:

GITLOW. Chief Commissar! Technically, that's a higher rank than mine. You should be pleased.

KORNFEDER. I am made to cut out ration coupons. ID stickers. Entry cards. Flyers. Flags. The charade is being turned into an amusement park.

April 12th. No surprises. They have decided to make the amusement park into a spectacle.

DECKER. Ben, we've had confirmation from the *Minneapolis Star*, the *Chicago Sun-Times* and the *Indianapolis Tribune* that their reporters will be there.

GITLOW. Thanks, John.

KORNFEDER. What the hell is going on? It seems a lot of planning's happening without me, all of a sudden.

GITLOW. Well, things are moving at a fast pace, Zack –

KORNFEDER. What's all this about the press?

GITLOW. How do you expect us to raise national awareness, without the national press being there? I'd say that's fairly elementary.

KORNFEDER. I know, of course, what will happen, as soon as those paperboys and ad-men and their cameras turn up. I know what the effect will be on the commitment of everybody involved.

April 17th. I have fought for the last remaining scrap of my plan to remain on the table – the arrest of the town's mayor. Ralph E Kronenwetter. It will be the start of the day. If I can leverage this – a demonstration of how to use force, to gain command, to stamp out freedom – then the day can still have some meaning.

> (**GITLOW** *walks towards the door of the Mayor's house. He knocks on the door.*)
>
> (*The door opens. The* **MAYOR** *stands there.*)
>
> (**GITLOW** *places a hand on the* **MAYOR**. *The* **MAYOR** *acquiesces, and is pulled away.*)

KORNFEDER. Cut.

It doesn't feel right.

GITLOW. What's wrong with it?

KORNFEDER. Knocking on the door undermines it.

GITLOW. What's wrong with that?

KORNFEDER. I think you can just force it open.

GITLOW. So, how do I do that, do I kick it down?

KORNFEDER. Maybe. Let's try it.

> *(They begin again.* **GITLOW** *walks to the door and mimes kicking it open, revealing the* **MAYOR.***)*

> *(***GITLOW** *places a hand on the* **MAYOR.** *The* **MAYOR** *acquiesces, and is pulled away.)*

Still not right.

GITLOW. I agree. I think it's a little extreme.

KORNFEDER. Just force it open with your shoulder.

GITLOW. How is that possible?

KORNFEDER. We'll work it out later.

GITLOW. Why can't I just knock?

KORNFEDER. That isn't what happens. They don't knock because they don't need to. Let's try it again.

And Mayor Kronenwetter, this time, try it without that…reaction when he enters.

> *(They begin again.* **GITLOW** *walks to the door, and mimes barging in.)*

> *(This time, the* **MAYOR** *doesn't respond.* **GITLOW** *places a hand on the* **MAYOR,** *who is pulled away.)*

Cut.

GITLOW. That didn't feel right. It was like dragging a sack of coal.

DECKER. I was just doing what I was told.

KORNFEDER. He was more believable. It's you who's the problem.

GITLOW. What do you mean?

KORNFEDER. You're too busy trying to act the hero. This isn't for the pictures.

GITLOW. I believe it is.

KORNFEDER. It can't be if we want people to believe what they're seeing. We don't believe there's any threat.

GITLOW. Exactly! That's why he should be resisting!

I think this would be easier if we did it with words. With the script that the Legion sent.

KORNFEDER. And I told you. We don't need it. The performance should be enough to carry it. They can add in script as narration.

GITLOW. Zack, let me try it. This isn't only your show.

KORNFEDER. Fine.

*(They reset. **GITLOW** approaches the door. This time, he knocks.)*

DECKER. Who's there?

GITLOW. Come out with your hands on your head.

DECKER. What for?

GITLOW. I represent the Council of People's Commissars. We're taking over this town.

*(The **MAYOR** opens the door.)*

DECKER. What do I say back.

GITLOW. Fight back.

KORNFEDER. Not physically.

*(The **MAYOR** settles for.)*

DECKER. Not in my town...you Commie...swine...!

> *(But he does not move.* **GITLOW** *places a hand on him and pulls him away. They look at* **KORNFEDER**.*)*

KORNFEDER. This is the worst version of them all, if I'm honest.

Why does he have to fight back?

GITLOW. You're asking me to break into the house of the Mayor – whom everyone in this town looks up to – and expect me to believe he wouldn't put up a fight? Nobody would believe that! It's ridiculous. It's disrespectful.

KORNFEDER. Disrespectful? You're here to kill him!

GITLOW. I'm here to arrest him.

KORNFEDER. Arrest is only the first beat. Then you kill him, and then the Chief Of Police, and the Chief Reverend, and everyone else in the town who tries to resist.

GITLOW. *(To the* **MAYOR**.*)* You'd put up a fight, wouldn't you? In his shoes?

DECKER. In whose shoes?

GITLOW. In yours. You wouldn't just let him walk into your property.

KORNFEDER. You would.

GITLOW. No you wouldn't.

KORNFEDER. Yes you would.

DECKER. Look, gentlemen, with respect, can we decide on a version and get along with it?

KORNFEDER. I'll tell you what the real issue, in all of this, currently. It's you, Gitlow.

GITLOW. What does that mean?

KORNFEDER. You're not even paying attention to the situation. Let me show you how to do it. This time, Mayor Kronenwetter, you say what feels right to you, in the moment, and I won't say anything.

*(They begin. **KORNFEDER** approaches the door much more slowly. When he reaches the door, he doesn't knock, or barge his way in. The **MAYOR** opens the door of his own accord.)*

DECKER. No. Please don't do this.

*(**KORNFEDER** enters the house with a slow, solemn intensity. The **MAYOR** speaks, pleads with him. **KORNFEDER** seizes him roughly, then pulls him out of the house. **KORNFEDER** pushes him down to his knees. The **MAYOR** whimpers for mercy. It all feels much more chilling.)*

*(**KORNFEDER** puts his fingers into the shape of a gun and points them to his head.)*

KORNFEDER. And this is where, if I had a gun, I would shoot him.

GITLOW. That won't be happening.

(The atmosphere changes to what it was before.)

KORNFEDER. Now, do you see what it needs to be? The whole encounter revolves around you, not him.

Your authority is enough to resolve our understanding. And our understanding is that in this society, we are powerless.

GITLOW. We're not going to be recreating one of your show trials for the papers, Zack. That isn't what America needs to see.

KORNFEDER. How else do you want them to understand the threat?

GITLOW. There's one thing, though, you've convinced me of from your little performance, though. You should be the one who does it, on the day.

KORNFEDER. Why? Because I was doing it correctly?

GITLOW. No, my dear friend.

Because you know how to do their accent, don't you?

*

KORNFEDER. What do you know of them? About any of this? For you, this is all just an act of make-believe. I am the one who has been there. I am the one who has been there. I am the one who'd seen. The towns. The soldiers. The gulags. Nadezhda and Leon. They were still there. I had not seen them for over ten years. Stalin. His face on every wall. Endlessly there. Always looking at you. What do you know? What gives you the right to imagine what has been the anchor around my heart?

His diaries don't record that. I just imagine him, wanting to say to the others. Needing to say it.

One of the only existing photos of Kornfeder is from the day itself. Behind him is a hand drawn poster, with a star and a hammer and sickle in front of it. In a circle around the star reads, Council of People's Commissars, United Soviet States of America. Kornfeder is standing with his arms crossed. He's glaring at the camera, lit from underneath, so it's glinting off his glasses and making him look, well, evil. It's clearly staged, like an ad for the thing that terrified him most in the world.

On April 30th, the day before, before an audience of select, invited press, there was a dramatisation of the Communists planning the takeover of Mosinee, performed by the anti-Communists planning the takeover of Mosinee. Kornfeder, Decker, Gitlow and Schweinler were all present.

By the time of the day itself, we lose track of Kornfeder's trail. His journal and personal accounts dry up. All that is left to us is the testimony of others. But I don't want to know what others have to say about him. I want to discover what he has to say for himself. I want to know that he took back control.

ACT THREE

GITLOW. Comrades! Tomorrow, our great Stalin leads us onwards to great triumphs. This war mad, blood thirsty fascistic American government little realises how close it is to its own doom. Long have the people of this land suffered under the yoke of capitalistic tyranny. Long have they been suffocated by ignorance and oppression. But friends, the hour of hope is yet at hand...

SCHWEINLER. What do you mean, Comrade General Secretary?

GITLOW. Allow me to elaborate, Comrade Schweinler. The sweet wine of vengeance is imminent. We count the hours when the poor and downtrodden workers will rise up and overthrow the whole, rotten regime of the United States.

DECKER. Glory to Stalin!

SCHWEINLER. Let his courage guide us!

GITLOW. Now, comrade Chief Commissar Kornfeder will reveal at last, his plan and vision for the coming insurrection.

KORNFEDER. Comrades.

There will be roadblocks set up. And then these will be followed by activists covering the town in banners and placards. And the Red Flag going up on public buildings. And social service

GITLOW. Comrade. A vision such as ours deserves a more vigorous deliverance, does it not?

DECKER. The people are hungry.

We will begin with the arrest by the Communist Combat Team of Mayor Ralph E Kronenwetter at his home on 303 Fourth Street.

We will then arrest Police Chief Carl Gewiss at his home on 301 Fourth Street.

There will be a violent seizure of power at Mosinee Paper Mill. There will be an arrest of all clergymen who will be sent to the prison camp on Beaver Street. There will be a seizure of the Public Library at the East End of Main Street. All literature, from the shortest pamphlet to the Bible itself, not on the officially mandated party line will be burned.

There will be a confiscation of firearms from the home of John Drengler at Drengler's Sporting Tavern. In fact there, will be a confiscation of firearms from every household and they will be seized and distributed to the soldiers of the Communist Army. There will be break-ins and inspections of homes at Princess Street, Green Street and Preston's Quality Bakery. But this will only be the beginning of it. All homes, across the entire town will be subject to inspection without notice and absolute obedience to the inspecting forces will be expected. Food, clothes, toys, furniture, decorations, any remote frivolity will be seized for redistribution. Social service classes will be established to teach the Communist line. The remotest disavowal or disobedience from the Party line will be met with severe physical discipline. The only option for food will come from distribution hubs that will be set up by the banks of the Wisconsin River. Black bread and borscht will be served and it will be disgusting and horrible, viler than anything else you've ever tasted in your life, and that will be the only option you have and you will relish it and tear it apart with your bare hands because of how hungry you are. Do you like the sound of that? Do you want more of that? Is that scary enough for you? Is that what you were imagining? Is that the kind of story you want? There will be a seizure of the Mosinee Paper Mill with the arrest of management and of any workers who do not co-operate. Any choice of employment will be abolished. The only labour will be hard labour. The only joy will be communal joy. The only comfort will be the Motherland. There will be a takeover of the Movie Theater, which will be enforced to present communist propaganda.ist propaganda.

GITLOW. Comrade. How will we achieve all this within one day?

KORNFEDER. The revolution will succeed because the revolution must.

*

KORNFEDER. As dawn rises, on International Worker's Day, the people of America awake to a new world.

A world of my making.

I wrap a band on my left arm. On it is the symbol of our movement. Of my army. Around me, my soldiers are doing the same. The show is beginning.

I begin to march towards the bridge. Roadblocks have been installed on 9th Street, Fremont St, 11th Street –

TOWNSPERSON. What's going on? Why aren't you letting me through?

Wait...wait...don't point that gun at me! I surrender!

KORNFEDER. Western Avenue, Pine Street , Creska Avenue

TOWNSPERSON. No, no, no, I don't have an entry permit, please just let me through, that's my mother's house! She doesn't know about any of this!

KORNFEDER. I watch as my soldiers adorn Main Street with the laurels of our movement.

SOLDIER. Take down that flag. We don't want to see that here. Any stars and stripes we see will be burned.

SOLDIER. Cut the telegraph wires. Ensure there's no outside interference.

SOLDIER. Open up! I demand you open up! In the name of the United Soviet States of America!

KORNFEDER. I watch as Francis Schweinler knocks on the door of the Lutheran Church.

SCHWEINLER. You're an enemy of the state, Father Bennett. I'm seizing this building and liquidating your role.

REVEREND. Mr Schweinler? Is that you? What...what are you doing? Why are you doing this?

SCHWEINLER. This regime has no tolerance for your parasitic creed.

REVEREND. Francis. Please! You're scaring me! I've known your family so long. Please have mercy.

KORNFEDER. It is as I have known all along. That this town was ripe for such an undertaking.

But, as I turn a corner on to Main Street:

REPORTERS. Give us a smile, will you Mr Kornfeder?

KORNFEDER. There is another army in Mosinee on this day, besides my own. It is this army that I will be in combat with today. The Army of the United States Press. And already they are crushing what I am trying to build.

REPORTERS. Could you tell us a little about what's going on?

TOWNSPERSON. I was just on my way to the grocers when I saw all these men in uniform turning up. It's terribly exciting!

REPORTERS. What's the card you're carrying?

TOWNSPERSON. It's a ration card. They sent it to us in the mail.

REPORTERS. What's the logo in the corner?

TOWNSPERSON. I don't know.

REPORTERS. Now can I just say, you look dashing in that military attire. Hold that pose for us, will you?

I don't see a flag or sign or anything outside your church, why is that?

TOWNSPERSON. We're the Catholic church, we don't really go in for this kind of thing.

REPORTERS. Sir, am I right in saying they tried to seize your firearms?

TOWNSPERSON. Not if I have any say over it.

KORNFEDER. I finally reach the house of the Mayor.

> (**KORNFEDER** *approaches the door. The* **MAYOR** *opens it.* **KORNFEDER** *opens it and seizes the* **MAYOR**. *He pulls him out.*)

CAMERAMAN. Cut. Can we go again on that, please? Needs a bit more life, fellas. And can we knock on the door?

> (*They reset. This time,* **KORNFEDER** *approaches again, but in a more heightened way. He knocks on the door. The* **MAYOR** *looks startled.* **KORNFEDER** *seizes him and pulls him out.*)

We're getting there, gentlemen, but you can really give it your all.

> (*This time, after the* **MAYOR** *opens the door –*)

Needs some dialogue, doesn't it folks? So we can understand the scene?

> (**KORNFEDER** *approaches the door, visibly unhappy. As he moves forward:*)

Give us a little more menace, won't you?

(**KORNFEDER** *resets and approaches. He knocks.*)

KORNFEDER. Come out with your hands on your head!

MAYOR. What for?

KORNFEDER. I represent the Council of People's Commissars. We're taking over this town.

(*As the* **MAYOR** *opens the door –*)

CAMERAMAN. Now I think we need that with your Soviet accent.

If that's not too much trouble to manage, Mr Kornfeder.

KORNFEDER. Come out with your hands on your head.

MAYOR. What for?

KORNFEDER. I represent the Council of People's Commissars. We're taking over this town.

(*The* **MAYOR** *opens the door.* **KORNFEDER** *pulls him out.*)

CAMERAMAN. Now let's get one more take with all of that please, folks. And this time, at the end, you can tell the Mayor where you're sending him, Zack.

As he approached the –

KORNFEDER. As I approached the Mayor again, I decide to take the scene into my own hands.

KORNFEDER. Come out with your hands on your head!

MAYOR. What for?

KORNFEDER. I represent the Council of People's Commissars. We're taking over this town!

(*The* **MAYOR** *opens the door.* **KORNFEDER** *pulls him out. Then –*)

*(He pulls a gun out and points it at the **MAYOR**. Suddenly, everything transforms on itself. Time freezes.)*

*(The **CAMERAMAN** steps forward. This time, they speak in their own accent, not an American one.)*

CAMERAMAN. *That's it. That's right. That's perfect. Keep that pose. That's just right.*

*(They move around the still image, photographing it. **KORNFEDER** turns and looks at them.)*

I think we've got it.

(Then –)

I don't think that's quite right.

*(Everything unfreezes. **KORNFEDER**'s gun has vanished.)*

GITLOW. We don't need Mr Kornfeder to pull him out, when we've got all these wonderfully menacing young soldiers accompanying him? Now let's get this in the bag sharply. Our next stop is the execution of the police chief.

KORNFEDER. Mosinee Town Square has been renamed to Red Square. Over a thousand townspeople have gathered and marched here. They marched with banners. They marched with placards. They marched with their fists raised to the skies.

I watch an eight-year-old boy waving a pistol in his hand with a smile on his face.

I watch a ten-year-old girl who is missing her mother.

I watch a forty-two-year-old man working at the paper mill wonder if this might be his opportunity for a raise.

KORNFEDER. A podium is set up in the Town Square. The Mayor is brought up.

MAYOR. Citizens of Mosinee. This town is now in the hands of the Council of People's Commissars. Our fates now belong to the United Soviet States Of America. I implore you to give yourselves over to the new regime, without resistance.

Now, it is my turn to address the crowd. I step up and find I cannot not speak. Time stands still. There is a hammer and sickle flying over the Square and it is the wrong way around.

I stare at the faces. They stare back at me. And all of a sudden I see a vision of my wife.

It's twenty years ago, and the two of us walking through Leningrad, before the war had reduced it to a charred cinder of rubble. It's our first time visiting the city. We walk along the Moyka River from Pevchevsky Bridge to the Red Bridge. The sun seems to dance off the water's edge. And we stop for ice cream at a stand and Nadezdha asks for two scoops, and we sit by the water and eat and I look at her and her lips are moistened with vanilla and she smiles at me and I think it is the most beautiful sight it is possible to witness.

I keep staring at the faces. I say nothing.

Finally someone boos, then someone else, then another voice and another and another.

Then I feel a firm hand on my shoulder. I am pushed aside. I turn and watch as Ben Gitlow takes the stand. He speaks and I hear:

GITLOW. The people, the workers, farmers and soldiers of America who have on this day triumphed over capitalistic rule, overthrown the bourgeois government of the United States, and seized power in their own hands, hereby decree with full and unlimited authority of the Council of Peoples Commissars the following:

All private property belongs to the people.

All land and subsoil resources belong to the people.

All industrial establishments, commercial enterprises and communication services belong to the people.

All transportation services, all energy services, all services that manage natural resources, belong to the people.

All debts, contracts of unequal service, and systems of rental dues between classes are abolished.

There will be full equality between all races of people. All systems of disenfranchisement and inequality in civil rights between races are abolished.

All systems of disenfranchisement and inequality between sexualities are abolished.

All unequal arrangements between genders are abolished.

All unequal arrangements between humanity and the natural world are abolished.

All facets of the military industrial complex are abolished.

All borders between sovereign states, nations, and peoples are abolished.

We will begin again, and understand ourselves and each other anew.

We will release the fear in our hearts and teach ourselves to hope again.

The future will belong to all.

KORNFEDER. They applaud.

Ben. Listen to me.

GITLOW. Go home, Zack. You're done here.

KORNFEDER. I thought we were comrades.

GITLOW. Comrades? You're a bit player, Zack. This is someone else's show now.

KORNFEDER. I walk down Main Street and survey the nightmare unfolding around me. Everywhere I only see the failure of my vision.

There is a queue for black bread and soup. The camera watches them.

TOWNSPERSON. Gee, this looks pretty horrid, Allen.

TOWNSPERSON. I know. If you don't want to eat it just head to Wausau. Their diners are still open.

KORNFEDER. A young man hands out copies of the official newspaper. It's labelled *The Red Star*. The camera watches him.

TOWNSPERSON. Extra! Extra! Soviets troops take over Mosinee!

TOWNSPERSON. Come on, you're pulling a fast one.

KORNFEDER. I walk past a man pitching a sign outside his property. It reads 'For Sale. Fifteen thousand rubles. Moving to Russia.' The camera watches him.

TOWNSPERSON. I didn't realise Barbara was throwing you out, Jim!

KORNFEDER. I walk past the concentration camp. There is a high, thin metallic fence drawn from one wall to another. It is topped with barbed wire. The inmates clutch the fence, just like in the photos from a few years ago. The camera watches them.

TOWNSPERSON. I'm gonna get off my knees, now, if you don't mind, they're a little weak.

TOWNSPERSON. Any of you got a smoke?

KORNFEDER. I walk into the movie theatre, past the admission booth. I walk over the soft carpet. I enter the auditorium.

The screen shows nothing but the photo of him. He, whose face never escapes me, who is always present even when my eyes are closed. His hair still combed back neatly. His mouth still covered by his brown moustache. His eyes still darting ceaselessly. They make contact with mine. The moustache curls upwards, and I finally see his mouth as he smiles.

STALIN. Why does any of it surprise you, comrade?

KORNFEDER. I don't reply.

STALIN. What did you think would happen when you turned your back on us and came to these shores? What did you expect to find? Rigour? Fortitude? Intellect? Because here they are free and there we are not? These average Americans cannot bring themselves to contemplate the darkness facing them.

KORNFEDER. I remain silent.

STALIN. And now you are trapped here with them, forever. While Nadezdah and Leon remain with me. You will never see them again. Unless you prove what remains of your worth to me, today. Unless you start your revolution. And how does that begin, comrade? Decapitate the power structure.

KORNFEDER. Behind me, I hear two voices:

We should have more days like this.

It's really brought together the community.

KORNFEDER. I stand and walk back out of the auditorium. Out of the movie theater. Back down Main Street.

When I reach the concentration camp, it is empty. Of course. The final event of the day is beginning and they want all the townspeople. The bonfire. Completely empty, apart from my target, the Mayor.

I represent the Council of People's Commissars. I'm taking over this town.

> (The **MAYOR** is scared. He tries to back away from **KORNFEDER** but **KORNFEDER** lunges for him. **KORNFEDER** grabs him and pulls him down. The **MAYOR** tries to crawl away from him. **KORNFEDER** keeps him pinned down.)
>
> (As this happens, the following:)

Across town, a congregation has gathered in Dessert Park. It is 7 p.m. and the day is coming to an end. All the placards and banners and flags and posters and ID cards and hats and scarves and toy guns and fake newspapers are being gathered on a pile ready for burning.

The townspeople are being addressed by Benjamin Gitlow.

GITLOW. Let this moment mark the end of the hideous indignity that we have suffered. We are purging this city of all evidence of our occupation by cleansing fire.

Remember, comrades – ours has only been a mild demonstration of our totalitarian enemy. It has been the purpose of the American Legion to depict life under communism so that through you who live in Mosinee, and through the press and newsreels, people who live everywhere may have brought to them the difference of life under communism and living in our beloved democracy.

> (**KORNFEDER** *pulls his gun out and starts shooting the* **MAYOR** *again and again.*)
>
> (**GITLOW** *lights the bonfire and all that has been created goes up in smoke.*)
>
> *
>
> (*We see recordings of interviews with townspeople, played by the company.*)

I was very small at the time but I do remember it. I was at the Catholic school and we weren't really involved, but some of the nuns, I think, Sister Grace, Sister Franklin, volunteered to take part, and they were taken to the prison camp by some nice young men dressed as soldiers.

I found out about it too late! I was out at Wausau picking up a delivery for my, uh, sister-in-law, when I bumped into Sandra Melchior, from the, uh, Parks department. And she says, hey, I've just come from Mosinee. There are these men dressed as soldiers everywhere! And I say, really? What for? And she says, it's, about Russia or something like that. And I decide to drive back to see what's up, and by the time I reach, it's all wound up.

I guess my main question was, who was it for? That's my question. Because it didn't seem like it was for us. It didn't even feel well managed. They pretty much swept in for a day, made a ruckus, then left us to clean up the mess after them. It's a shame, 'cause there's a version that could've much more educational, like at the High School, or something.

What do I think about it now? I haven't thought about it for over thirty years.

It's a shame about Mayor Ralph, he was very sweet. Was always getting involved with community events, so no surprise he wanted to be a part of it. He was only in his late 40s! Far too young to have a heart attack. He'd had an accident while fishing the week before, which maybe triggered something. And then I think all the excitement of the day maybe just got to him.

The men who ran it, they didn't seem too interested in talking to any of us. The only people I remember, uh, talking to is the newspaper men. Or some of the boys handing out the fake flyers and leaflets. I asked one of them, what do you think of all this. And he said I think it's swell.

No, I don't think that name means anything. Who was that?

Yes, the gentleman in a bowler hat! I saw him give a speech at the Town Square. Then I remember seeing him wandering around Main Street, going up to the roadblocks. Seemed to be inspecting them. He seemed, I dunno, grumpy? Like the day wasn't going how he wanted it.

I think it was quite a nice thing, truth be told. Mosinee's had some bad luck since then. The Paper Mill closed down in the 70s, and people just started leaving after that. So for there to be a day where the town became famous, I don't know, that feels like a nice thing for us.

*

Sometimes, I ask myself, what was the twentieth century really like? And then I remember, that from the beginning, when John Decker potentially happened to be at Joe McCarthy's rally and potentially first had an idea, to May 1st 1950, which definitely happened, was three months. Three months from idea to outcome. Try and imagine something like that today.

As Kornfeder's day began, his steps vanished before us. All we could do was step into his imagination. But his imagination wasn't enough. America was still unreachable to him, so all he could do was invent an ending. So what you just saw was our own interviews with the townspeople of Mosinee, to help us see the day through their eyes. Our final stab at imagining America.

Joseph Zack Kornfeder died thirteen years after the events at Mosinee. His remaining writing continued to stress the importance of vigilance against infiltration of American society by fifth columnists, and the potential for subversion from within. But after America invaded Korea, and then Vietnam, all his talk sounded hollower and hollower, and less and less attention was paid to it. We don't know if he ever reunited with his wife and child.

There's one other photo of him from the day, alongside the evil-looking one. It's taken a few moments before, or after, the latter. Behind him is the same hand drawn poster, with a star and a hammer and sickle, with the Council of People's Commissars written on it. But on this one, he looks more relaxed. Maybe like he's on the verge of a smile. Like he's at peace with events. We didn't know what to do with that picture, but we felt like we ought to share it with you now.

Within the Day under Communism, the real life Soviet Union had sent a reporter from their news agency, undercover, to relay the events to Moscow. So, amongst a day of fake Communists pretending to be real, directed by two real Communists who are now fake pretending to be real again, there was a real Communist faking at not being a Communist while actually being one.

This is what he reported back when he returned to Moscow.

EDITOR. Welcome back, comrade. I hope the West hasn't been too much of a lure for you!

REPORTER. Thanks, comrades. It's been quite an adventure but I have missed the Motherland. Things are a bit more...grounded here.

EDITOR. Your last report sounded pretty intense. What was this thing you attended? And where on earth was it?

REPORTER. It was in Wisconsin. The Midwest. Basically... our Siberia. And yes, they were putting on an event that tried to replicate what our lives are like.

EDITOR. Wow.

REPORTER. Yep.

EDITOR. Well, this is well-timed comrade, as we are planning a series of educational events here, about what life is like in the West. Under the capitalists. So your expertise would be much appreciated.

REPORTER. OK sure. Where are you at with it?

EDITOR. Ideally, it shouldn't be a museum piece, or a presentation, or lecture. We want something that feels like it's happening in the moment, like it's live. We want an audience there watching. We want there to be a beginning, middle, end, and for it be contained in a short timeframe. We want to follow both a recognisable character and an entire community, an entire system of thinking, and an entire way of being. We want there to be a sense of confrontation with how we think about others. We want a sense of tremendous hope and irrevocable loss. We want to feel happy and to feel sad too. We want to hold space for ambiguity, and uncertainty, and for imagining. We want to doubt.

> *(As the **SOVIET EDITOR** continues listing his intentions for the Day Under Capitalism, the lights start to fade, and Fleetwood Mac play 'Don't Stop'.*)*

The End

---

* A licence to produce *THE MOSINEE PROJECT* does not include a performance licence for 'Don't Stop'. The publisher and author suggest that the licensee contact PRS to ascertain the music publisher and contact such music publisher to license or acquire permission for performance of the song. If a licence or permission is unattainable for 'Don't Stop', the licensee may not use the song in *THE MOSINEE PROJECT* but should create an original composition in a similar style or use a similar song in the public domain. For further information, please see the Music and Third-Party Materials Use Note on page iii.

Milton Keynes UK
Ingram Content Group UK Ltd.
UKHW020250270724
446175UK00010B/233

9 780573 000645